# STORMY
# SUNSHINE

# STORMY SUNSHINE

## The Poetry Experience
## Of a Lifetime

## Regina Medina Alvarado

ISBN PAPERBACK: 979-8-9875779-0-5
Library of Congress Control Number: 2023915474
First Edition Paperback: March 17, 2023
Las Vegas, Nevada. United States of America

## DEDICATION

To my readers,

Savor this slowly

And

To my children,

My love for you is eternal.

"It was as if...

*...every journalist and*

*every reporter*

*had fallen ill.*

*They sent a poet*

*instead.*"

# CONTENTS

# CONTENTS

❖ CHAPTER TWO

# CONTENTS

Though we may bask under the comfort of the warm sun, every now and then our very own stormy sunshine of turmoil unexpectedly appears.

**OUR LIVES ARE LIKE THE FOUR SEASONS, FILLED WITH SUNSHINE, GLADNESS, TRAGEDY AND MADNESS.**

**No one escapes.**

# CHAPTER ONE

## SUNBURN
### EARTH'S CRY

# EARTH'S CRY

Discontent

Anguish

Injustice

Solitude

Sorrow

# THINGS I'LL NEVER FORGET...

A hot summer day on the California coast...it must have been an innocent 86-degree, cloudless sky. The salty fresh air filled my lungs with invigoration. Relief from city smog and noise was long overdue, that lucky-to-be-alive feeling coursing through my veins, wine goblet in hand, and not a care in the world...

What time was it?
Who cares!
Sunglasses looked good on everyone...

Four hours later...

102-degree skin boiled over
No shade
No shield
No mercy

What was I thinking...

The sun obeys no one.

# SUNBURN

IT'S UP TO ALL
Each one of us
To measure care and detriment
Avoid the scorching solar flare
Escaping its harsh punishment

From humble loyals to crowned royals
*-Avoid the bright white fire-*
Our daily dose
If sunlight chose
Could blind and pierce us tired

So powerful, it makes the moon
Go hide in wait 'til daylight ends
But when they meet at the eclipse:

...a celebration of two friends

# HOURGLASS UNCERTAIN

I don't know how I feel today
Uneasiness remains
An awkward feeling deep within
Perhaps in bed I'll stay

Alone in my dread
Heavy doubt--I can't shed
A cough, a faint pulse
I'm feeling half-dead

The view's not as bright
My whole life:
    ONE LONG RUN
The start line behind in the haze
Now long gone
I didn't even toil in the sun
A feeling as weary
As post-marathon

Like a drain that won't stop
My life force—out of gas
The mirror yells,
"Hourglass, you're going too fast!"

Can't seem to catch up
I try not to gasp
Abyss of affliction
Release your tight grasp

I'm turning my face towards
A bright ray of hope
Picking clovers of four leaves
With red wine to cope

Can't wait for tomorrow
Right now, I'll just say
I'll be careful and grateful
I woke up today

# FLAMINGO VACATION

Beyond city smog
And fast-moving cars
Away from streetlights
No buildings, no bars
No people, no paper
No industry toughness
No artificial rules
To impede nature's justice

There exists such a place
As special as gold
Where few of us wander
Away from Earth's cold

Here, gone is the stress
Of our man-made delusions
A tropical paradise
A floral illusion

A rare hidden gem
A distant place for the bold
In a cool inland lake
Or a mangrove watering hole
Where blue skies do hover
Over soft, sandy islands
Where tropical palms sway
Away from the dry land

Vast spaces surrounding
The pink colony
Flocks hidden domain
A place to roam free
Away from the eagle
Who is part of the chain
But our man-made pollution:
That's the real threat to them

With their numbers declining
I must sound the alarm
To change the set patterns
That result in their harm

Can we ever imagine
Our land without wonders
Their beauty as brilliant
And striking as thunder

A flamingo vacation
How I envy their flight
The ultimate paradise
I glimpse Heaven's delight

Who will help me to save
Earth's most wondrous feature?
So cool, so laid-back
This fantastic pink creature

# FLAMINGO FOREVER

# CALM BEFORE THE STORM

It was the first day of spring
2020 AD
I glanced above
Not a plane in sight
In the calm, still painting
Of a light blue sky
Billowy clouds formed
Their natural high

There contained a peaceful stillness
A somber 2020 vision clearness
A hush so foreign
To my once-busy ears
Alone stood a tall, lanky tree
That had not spoken in years

When at once came a sound
From way up high
Celebrating the return
Of his reign in the sky

Adorned with the freshness
Of March greenery
In the middle of this
Tall, tall tree
Proud songbirds'
A cappella-
Singing a melody
Just for me

*Hardly any traffic...*

## LETTER TO THE UNSEEN

We thought 2020 would surely be the best
Excitement of dreams and pride filled our chests
Unexpected demise of our confident role
Stirring our blindsided souls

We didn't expect you, but
You sure came quick
Like a blink, and a wink
Like a light switch flip

Like slithering smoke
In a wayward sprint
No sirens of warning
No perilous hint

You spread your wings wide
Canvassed and hurled
Gave mercy to none
And shook the whole world

The streets and our cities
Turned silent
An eerie dark feeling
No one to confide in
Sheer uncertainty
A bit like roulette
Adhering to droplets
In planes and in jets
Our fresh oxygen tank
In the sky--you hijacked
No ransom exchange
Just a silent attack
Pervading the airwaves
Saturating our airways
Like a sudden chokehold from the back

So greedy, so mean, infectious stream
Invisibly present, a presence unclean
Silent, quietly spreading in spray
Our lives jolted...we trembled, we prayed

We quietly waited
For a sound that made sense
But the tide brought instead
*A thick,*
       *Daunting*
             *Silence*

# POETRY'S DESPAIR

The painter stopped painting
The writer is waiting
The flowers are dying
Their color is fading

The instruments down the hall
All abandoned
The pilots are resting
Since all planes have landed

Came a shadowy aura
An invasive gray wave
Unnerving our feelings
Like visiting a grave

Inhaled a world
Of nervous energies
A Groundhog Day year
An apocalyptic mystery

# FIRE IN PARADISE, CA

Is it safe to open the windows yet?
Even though I live far away
My eyes: red and weary
From the long reach
Of traveling smoke
Gasping, inescapable
Turbulent gray
Children no longer play outside
Fearing unseen danger lurking by
Their homes meant to shelter
To protect each life
Now all that's left are ashes
Memories, strife

I don't dare imagine
It was a lifeline implored
As the blaze filled the sky
With sounds of roar
A dangerous site
You could not hear the shouts
Of desperate ones yelling:

"Help us get out!"

Counted 85 souls
Missing from the rest
A million prayers whispered
"We've lost our best"
Like Sodom and Gomorrah
-A grim story to tell-
Our beloved Paradise
Has now burned to hell

More than anything,
I ponder upon the
Quagmire of it all...

- PARADISE LOST -

A divine warning?
A foreshadowing of things to come?
Is anybody listening?

# A PLACE TO CALL HOME

We worked hard all of our lives...
Then died

Yet, life itself felt like living a thousand deaths
Seems all the others got:

    The longest, lucky straw
    The quickest, richest draw
    Gifted genuine stones
    Never fooled by fool's gold

The shortest straw
Bank overdraw
The bag of coal
Hard winter's cold
Expired goods, ill health
No wealth
Tumbleweeds
Hunger's greed
Life's never-ending needs
Was left for you
And me...

A constant yearning
For a place of our very own
Without a non-stop mortgage drain
To see the end of spending pain
In a home where children
Take refuge and feast, then
Leave your empty nested
Home converts to
Final days of resting
Awaiting the imminent path
Of life's finality

Seems we were always
Put through the wringer
Like sand, our good fortune
Escaped our fingers

For so many
Hard-working
Folks today, the
American Dream
Slipped away...

## MELTING POT

# 1886

## Lady Liberty

## WELCOMED ALL

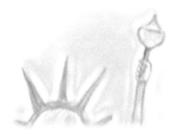

# 2022

## Lady Liberty

## QUITS

"Actually, I did not quit. I was cancelled."

Another casualty of

# The Great Resignation

# THE LAND OF PLENTY

They named her *America:*
The land of plenty
Once a safe harbor of serene homes
Of playgrounds, of melancholic days...
Swept away, like broom dust

Now, something more insidious roams

We have a lot of freedom here
Take freedom of speech, for instance
We are free to speak whatever is on our mind
People do it all day long, everywhere

...I long to hear the laughter of children

Instead, media sounds blast out serenity
Laced with the hailstorm of society's mood
Deep sadness pervades in the clouds
That once sang, "This land is your land"
Showers of radicalism, racism and rudeness
More popular than niceness
All clothed in "right of free speech" attire

Yes, there is PLENTY in the land of plenty

# I DO NOT WISH FOR RICHES

My wish is
For racism and hate
To fade away into oblivion's nest
Replaced by
A "MONTREAL AGREEMENT"
Of understanding & forgiveness

To see hate
Turn into *help*
*Happiness*
*Hope*

Stopping the hate starts
with every one of us,
there is no other way.
There's a creeping in my bones
as a menacing shadow shouts,
'Judgment Day is on the way'

# MERRY GO ROUND

Merry go round and
Round and round
Spin round 'til you're blank
You'll be upside down
Watch that fresh keen smile
Turn a cold hard frown
Flying up really high
Then life on the brink
As your ICE-COLD DRINK
Knocks you down

If you're rich or you're not
Who's to say you'll escape
Lose a hat or a crown
It will steal your great
Seal your fate
Make your good luck dissipate
Then laugh at your face
Like a doomed blind date
...but don't let that make you hate
(Because it's only temporary)

I know we all struggle, but
I'm crushed once again
Bumpy roads through the miles
Through the hills and the bends

I'm doing my best to put on a smile
Hide the sadness and tears
Running through my veins
I fear this may drive me insane

All we ask is 'let us be'
It's everyone's right to
Maintain dignity
Trapped once again
We just want to be free
From the heartache and pain
Of a jailhouse stay
They got quotas to meet
With batons they will beat
Or maybe detain us to burn in the heat
The heat of an officer's bone-hard knee
On the heat of the black tar street

M-G-R here's the heartache once more...

They say that the pain
Will take off like a plane
Faraway it will go
I'll be happy again
But the pain, no one said
Is as heavy as led
As I sink to the ground
Super-glued to the land
Where's a helping hand when
I need it...

*Another round and this torment abounds*
*Praying for a better life and town*

I'm glad the night has finally arrived
Time to leave all my tears on my pillow
Then I'll dream that we're blessed
Give my heartache a rest
As we swing on my tall weeping willow

...yes we'll swing on my tall weeping willow...

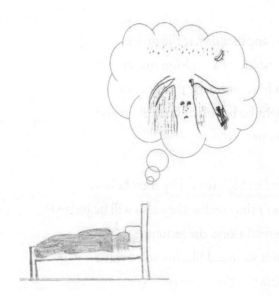

# TWO FOR ONE SPECIAL

It was the day of sentencing
The judge read aloud the punishment
Smooth words rolled off
His iron tongue like syrup
No hesitation, not a wince

Just another day at the office
In the life of a decision maker
On his man-made throne, but
Might he be full of human errors?
Like us?

Held in high regard by men below...
Don't they realize they also will be judged?
He read aloud the sentence
But it sounded like his voice was a
*...faint,   far   away   echo...*
Am I lightheaded, or
Was I just hit in the gut?
Is this really happening?
A surreal daytime nightmare

"State prison for you, young man
10 years plus..."
He said with the same tone of
Sending a kid off to summer camp

The judge lost not a second more
Moved on to the next case
Certainly not a second of sleep
To be lost over our loss...
We saw that in his stoic face

After all, it was
Not his son sent away

Wise as they are, you would
Think a judge understands
With those condemning words
*HE ALSO SENTENCED ME*

"Stop the drinking," they said,
"I will, once my heartache stops
Or maybe when I'm dead."

# MAMA BEAR GETS MAD

DON'T TELL ME
To stop drinking
Or crying for my sons
The ones that you locked up
For admiring shiny guns

See, it's what they've played with
Since the dawn of the cowboy
They just want to imitate
A hero with a lifelike toy

Since fast horses and hats
Can't compete with smoke pistols
Nor caplets or water guns
Made of cheap plastic crystal

I will forever love and
Defend my sons
Who've been MISLED and GROOMED
Into admiring the cowboy's gun

Let's play fair:
Lock 'em ALL up today!
There's a long list of offenders
Including the N R A
The ones that hunt caribou
The ones that sport duck
The killer of bears
You must lock 'em ALL up!

And because Mr. Officer
It is what you like to do:
Lock yourself away
You carry a gun too

# MY JANUARY SON

My once tiny baby boy
Arrived a heap of bursting love
My January son, Bebito
Sent to us from Heaven's trove

Could not wait to hold you close
Grappling tightly Heaven's vine
Anticipating your sweet laughter
And your smile of pure sunshine

I regret I was not brave enough
To pull you in a better direction
To spare you from the stumbles learned
From the errors of our reflection

How can years pass so quickly?
How can time fly by, not last?
Like the turning of the page
Our short youth left us all too fast

Never saw the weighted measure
A SHORT TIME ASSIGNED, said page
Unforeseen by anyone
Even by the wisest sage

I chant our name aloud with FREEDOM
Feel my presence, I'm there too
In your shadow, see my image
I will always stand by you

Time, injustice, pain, or distance
Can't declare us lone or distant
Imprisoned bodies in a cage
Chained forever? Nonexistent

The lessons may have beat us
But I know they won't defeat us
Even when it turns to rain
Always something left to gain

A river's cry detoured through my eyes
A deluge soon to pass
Welcome nature's nourishment
Come rewards of emerald grass

In your time of cloudy sadness
Look above at parting skies
See the endless love I send
To turn your sorrow into
Laughter's reign

Welcome every sunray's visit
Shining beams stand strong and bright
Breaking clouds will erase scowls
And we'll bask in rainbow's light

# CITIZENS ENRAGED

The skies are still filled with smoke
Not just from the nearby fires
Fuming, angry smoke radiates from
Discontented, enraged citizens
Communities of lives rightfully
Gathered to protest against
An armed operative, frightfully
The most powerful gang
In the land

Of which SOME have the audacity
To label those with unmatched skin
Who don't dress, speak
Or inherit like them
'A threat to society'
Instantly slapping on cuffs
Getting away with treating people rough
Perhaps blinded by intolerance, bias, or haste?
Pouring money into helicopter swarms
So expensive—what a waste!

Imagine hanging out in your grandmother's
backyard, cell phone in hand: Now, imagine that it
suddenly ends...

This young man faced the stronghold of two
"militant-like invaders with trained intelligence in
deciphering a situation" with a cell phone. Lights
in his eyes. Scared.
Wait, my bad...I'm sorry...
The two officers who chased him—*they* feared for
their lives, it was said.
A young unarmed black man
Holding a cell phone in his hand
Their target eyes only 16 feet away
Shattered many lives that day
Did anyone in charge shout the command,
"Stop! Drop what is in your hand!"
Decisions prevailed much too fast
GET EVERY OFFICER AN EYE EXAM

Might a Taser have spared his life?
When will compassion and skill suffice?

Since when have guns resembled cell phones?
Where is the technology?
...the close up image from a drone?
The job requires courage
With valor and nerves of steel
Instead we're seeing impulsive ones who
Hastily exercise their license to kill

So if you see guns pointing straight at you
Lift your arms up high, towards God
-Don't run-
Speak up nice and loud and clear
Or they'll say you carry a gun

SIGN OF THE TIMES

# I
# HAVE A

## Question: Why are

### They Protecting

Replaceable objects

With More Passion than

Protecting an

Irreplaceable life?

# MERCURY RESERVED

STOP!
Yelled the cop
Sweeping the streets of the
Under-served
Treating the citizens as
Un-deserved
Always willing to
Over-serve
Giving himself a raise
On overtime self-served

Target eyes like scopes
Eagle eyes on prey
A mother's constant prayer:
    DON'T TAKE MY CHILD AWAY
It's their time to stretch their wings
Singing all the way to eighteen
A youthful time to laugh and explore
*THIS GOD. GIVEN. FREEDOM. WE. ADORE.*

A chance to earn a decent wage
In a car without a tow

But the doors of opportunity
Are too far from the poverty row

It's reserved for those in homes
Of fancy etched glass doors
Who waltz upon their daydreams
On spacious quartz dance floors

We do not stand a lucky chance
Against militant-styled "Robocops"
Where's the safety in safety officer?
Maintaining power at the top

Stripping rightful citizens
Of their right to bear arms
By trigger-happy peace officers
Who shatter peace in a bullet run

Invading citizens' safety nests
Homes without the glam or glitz
Yet, these home invaders in blue insist
They are the "people's" patriots

"STOP!"
I yelled at the cop
Please think before you shoot
Stop and look at me, your target
A member of the human group

This is not the Olympics
Not the time to take first place
No quick draw, or you'll get the short straw
Please put away the mace

No gold medal for legalized killers
Go instead play your video game thrillers
You're intelligent; please learn, discern
Don't fall into disgrace

Did you know your shiny badge
Can create a sickening fear
Capable of causing hurricanes
Of a million mother's tears?

There is a place like Mercury
For those enjoying hate instead
A place of equal reprimand
Divine punishment, dread

It was formed by our Creator
The one we call *The Most High*
For punishers without compassion
With hate and evil in their eye

The eye of pride and racism
Who behave worse than a beast
Those sinful souls will perish
In darkness to never cease

Bullets are never the answer
To get someone to change
That's why a place like Mercury is reserved
For those relishing in others pain

# ZERO TOLERANCE

# AMERICAN DAUGHTER

She was the bravest of young soldiers
This young woman who joined Fort Hood
She could have been anything she wanted
In America, she knew you could

Her footsteps were very humble
Much too honorable for the Hood
Where she joined that army jungle
In a place where evil stood

Strong and solid was her vision
Emulating a true leader
Planned to guard the gated nation
But instead, caged in with cheaters

Caught off guard against a villain
Lusting after her fine beauty
Then a haunting turn of fate
When she vanished from her duty

Her sister's voice, harrowing, like an alarm
Her firm words did pierce our hearts
How in God's name can this happen?
On a base where laws impart

A soldier's message echoes clearly
Reaching far beyond the grave:

> *"Stand guard. Maintain.*
> *Muster furiously.*
> *Be brave.*
> *You have a voice, now use it!*
> *You have one life:*
> *Don't let anyone abuse it!"*

A promotion into Heaven's book
Leaving far behind Earth's gloom
A budding royal rose in camouflage
Crushed before her full life bloom

"Aztec Princess" Illustration. Unknown Artist. 2010

Elevated to an Aztec Princess
Adorned in graceful gold attire
Forever blessed in calm directions
Eternity under God's protection

Dedicated to the
Memory of

## Vanessa Guillen

Brave American soldier
Daughter, sister, friend
Child of God

Her life was taken
At an American Army Base:
Fort Hood, Texas

We pray for the family's long-suffering
May they find peace knowing
Vanessa's spirit is with God

May this never happen again

# HOUSE SLAVE

So much to do for all but me
I want 'remote control'
Limited access for one, just me
*How does it feel to be free?*

How about a name change, please?
Reasons written in my parched diary
A one-way ticket to far away
A flight out of poverty

Get dinner prepared
Make sure the cooking's done right
Don't go over budget
It's as tight as a kite

It's hard to create a good meal
Tasty and light
Every day after day
Repeat night after night

With no time for me, not a minute to lose
In the constant drudgery of "non-stop to do"
Too busy working, so these gifts go unused
My God-given gifts are my birthright shoes

Lots of effort, no helper
It's been a long, useless time wishing
I know I lack the Midas touch
Needed for success in the kitchen

*What good is a bucket list anyway,*
*When all you get is a mop bucket*

I'd gladly give my hat away
To one better suited for this vessel
My hands were made for other things
Yes, things unimportantly special

# CHOKEHOLD

You used to be strong
Then along came one stronger
You used to be cheerful
Seems now you're just tearful

Can't go anywhere
To mingle or share
Can't polish your nails
Won't color your hair

So full of resentment
You stare at the walls
Drenched in regret
Can't answer, don't call

Who knew that a promise
Could be just like a prison
For some, love is blind
A distortion, a prism

You're living for one
Oh yes, he's the one
The one controlling
Your freedom, your fun

Warned that he'd hate
Your passion and peers
Now it all seems
Your days are as years

Like quicksand you're stuck
On a super-glued ride
A rough rollercoaster
Deceived by the glide

So many near misses
Low hisses in kisses
Take a close look:
Is he mad or malicious?

He's clever; he'd never
Admit jealousy
Instead, he'll declare
He lets you roam free

Only a miracle
Can save both your souls
Yours from his grip
His from the coals

# RUN

"You're saying, dear friend,
He's out of control?
All I can tell you is
Save yourself, go"

                    "We all know that
                    Heeding a warning is right,
                    But once the storm passes
                    We don't even fight"

"Just look at the pattern
It's always a cycle
He goes from Prince Charming
To Mr. Hyde Psycho"

                    "I have his young children,
                    That should keep him gentle"

"Go tell it to cousin-
Shot down near the mantle...

Her three little children
Had witnessed the horror
Then, orphaned, were driven
Away in the Explorer...

How many glasses must
He first shatter
Before you realize his anger
Is a serious matter?"

*RUN*

# CHOKEHOLD'S END

All over the world is the
Suffering of women and girls
Treated as second-class citizens
Sometimes more like slaves
Or rag dolls made to absorb
The ignorance of rage

A 2020 worldwide search = 66,000
Those statistics are daunting!
Sometimes right under our nose
A woman's cries for help unnoticed
Well, I'm here to put out a notice

What will it take to permanently end
The domineering culture of
"Tough macho," it's haunting!
Clear rules, not only in school, but
In homes, by anyone, teach everyone
Every child, at every inch and every mile
Violence against women not only affects
The victims, left behind are entire families
Relatives, close and distant

I am haunted by far too many
Names listed in obituaries
I cringe each time I see the grief of
Another headstone in a cemetery

I can't believe they had to come up with
A new word for this crime:
"Femicide" - look it up
We are all at risk: Our moms, grandmothers
Daughters, sisters, cousins, aunties, friends-
The list of those affected includes men

There are far too many "Gabby Petito's" out there:
Lacy Peterson; Deanna Cook; Mona Heydari;
Beloved cousin Christina was not able to escape;
Sweet Desiree Favela married the wrong type of
cop--that grimly sealed her fate

Women and girls have a long standing dream
How much longer must we wait?
To finally live in a world that ends
Aggression, violence, murder, and hate!

## WINE'S RIPPLE EFFECT

E vil water...
      *Twisted*
          *Smooth*
             *Seductive*
                *Deceptive...*

Like a fake smile

Enticing...
Filled with promises
Of enlightenment
Of good feelings
Of good time dealings

You select your glass
Not just any glass

Your *favorite* glass

Tall, crystalline and sleek
Will it be red, white, or pink?
You lovingly kiss the liquid
Caressed by your inner cheek

The delicious drink flows
Flows deep into your soul
Like an injection, a one-way party
Invisible evil ripples within
Soaking every portion of your flesh
Permeating every vein
Absorbing all of the toxins
The oncoming tsunami is imminent:
Get ready for the crash

Vanished is the wall of inhibition
Feelings of freedom entrance
Followed by the frantic, endless
Whirlwind of dance, dance, dance!
Suddenly you feel half your age
You are deaf: TURN UP THE MUSIC
Your words: loud, repetitive

Like a raging river
There is no turning upstream
No going back-ever-forever written
Into the historical sands of time...

As certain as tomorrow's sunlight
The pounding ache in your head arrives
The nauseating smell of everything
*Did I offend anyone?* -remains unanswered
Doubt, regret, and shame follow
Recall does not exist
The memory door forever closed

Young onlookers recall, recant
The intriguing moment in time that was you
Yet, was not...
This unbelievable tale is
Certainly their imagination
No way!
Not I!

Not even a bath can remove the shame, nor
Smells of that forgettable night

The delicious drink flows
Flows deep into your soul
It would have been much better
*If I had just said no*

# DESTINATION: NOWHERE

When good measure is forgotten
Our good fortune turns out rotten


DRINKING
+ DRIVING

= DISASTER

-The importance of doing the math

## KARMA'S REVENGE

Just when I thought
Things couldn't get worse
What seemed like a nightmare
Was really a curse

Trampled again by
Life's sharp torpedoes
Invisible pangs
As prickly pear needles

Don't ever tempt karma
Just stay in the right
Do no wrong to others
Don't ever pick fights

If you don't believe me
Just keep your eyes open
I pray you stay safe
Keep wishing, keep hoping

I tell you I know this
I confess my wrongs
I knew it would catch me
It didn't take long

This circle of life
The cycle of death
I won't cross my fingers
I can't hold my breath

Instead I'll tell others
To help them see
How karma pays back
For our harsh revelry

Let's always think twice
Before taking that leap
A leap that will certainly
Sow what you reap

## TOO BUSY TOO LITTLE TOO LATE

"Where are you going?
Here's your assignment,"
Said Mother Destiny

"Sorry, I've no time
To listen to you
I know what I'm doing
I know where I'm going
Life is a carnival
I'm breaking in new shoes!"

Now, time came to pass
Maybe 20 years or more
Needing advice from her mother
She knocked on her door

In front stood a stranger who said,
"Do come in
I'm here as your mother's
Pretend next of kin
She left far away
Beyond that big hill
Here's something she left you-
I think it's her will."

It wasn't her will
She had nothing to give
Instead was advice on
How to best live

It was no longer needed
I had just realized
My selfish ways taught me
By way of surprise
To never neglect our
Parents who love us
The only ones loyal
Who put nothing above us

# WINGS CLIPPED

In the mirror was somebody
If I close my eyes, I see
A strange relic
From the past
Of a faded memory

A memory of conquering
Mountains, hills, and trees
Laughter was my daily habit
When my youth was here with me

My young heart was
Strong, courageous
An honest, open book to read
My defense: an unseen guardian
Always one to fight and lead

Brave young wings
Spanned untamed space
Strong legs outran every race
Danced a song with style and grace
In a time that cherished haste

Many things have changed since then
Time will steal your youth, your bold
As a stone house surely crumbles
Seasons do declare us old

Not a thing to do to stop it
See, it's always nature's way
Nature's fury wins each time
Wings no longer fly away

# REPLACED

Wrinkled and tired were their eyes
The eyes of the wise
Laced with tears that fell between
The crevices of skin aged dry

I heard one whisper
*How fast go the years*
They gently declined
Fancy party invites
Citing arthritic bones
The fright of surprise
And sudden loud noise

They did slow down
Moved out of the way
Made room for the young
Generation, those with
Exuberance, drive and
Endless motivation

Youthful, sparkling eyes
Filled with eagerness
And anticipation
Of the exciting unknown
Of new sensations

All dressed in their finest
Feeling immortal, no fear
Delighting in nightfall
All smiles, no tears
Fast moving lives
Too busy to hear

While raising their glasses
To bountiful cheers
When suddenly time stops:
They too have grown old
Now slow is their pace
Matching tortoise and owl

# FATHER'S EYES

So it is, we hold our memories
Childhood's timeless, carefree phase
Grandest summers filled of fun
Were the best of our best days

From the screams of romping children
As we heard the last school drill
To the pumpkins that we hollowed
In the late October chill

But those things that I recall
Here's a thing remembered most
Well it's not a thing at all
Reappears just like a ghost

In my father's two keen eyes
Deep emotions did reveal
His eyes reflected-
At times protected-
Or cut through you like steel

The apple of his eyes
The best of him I'd seen
I was his only daughter
Like his mother, named me queen

His was a special glance, and rare
A twinkling quiet softness
Shined the sweetest tenderness
Under his blue-collar roughness

Then settled in a glacial glance
That hardened icy stern
Peering through the curtains
Screening visitors affirmed

He was solid in his dealings
He had power in his stare
One straight look that said it clearly
*DO NOT ENTER—*
*DON'T YOU DARE*

There was also disappointment
Followed by the tears of pride
Tears that never fell, but rather
Glistened pain and scorn inside

Friends and family, none excluded
Lived to see his stumbled lessons
Many cherished goals eluded
Pain did overshadow blessings

With the days and years, his passing
You would think pain disappears
Tears still fall down from my eyes
Time again, tears reappear

Hard to swallow when I smell
It's the scent of tears, unique
One I recognize so well
Like the dampness on my cheek

Father's eyes have closed forever
But they'll always be with me
Because when I close my eyes to rest
It's his twinkling eyes I see

****

It is a strange and lingering regret when a loved one passes away, without a service to say goodbye, without a headstone or a grave to visit...without having said words a loved one wants to hear:

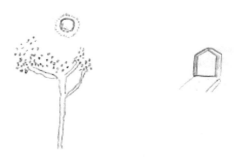

"Father, we love you always...
Rest in peace with our Lord
Until we meet again."

# IMMORTAL

Our lives begin alike
All innocent and pure
From golden days of youth
Adulthood is the allure

Then death knocks on your door
Uncertain who'll be next
We're all on Reaper's list
Every one of us is hexed

The pain we feel inside
Our lives, sometimes unsure
Life's imminent torpedoes
So difficult to endure

That's why we all do stumble
That's why some drink for cheer
We're striving for God's love
His mercy's always near

Still, we wouldn't trade this trip
We want to ride this ride
Grim Reaper's never hip
From death we cannot hide

And even though we're scared
While walking the same line
We'll do our best while here
Enjoying God's sunshine

Your tired soul is at peace now
And in the Lord's good hands
Forever in our hearts
No matter where we land

You've won the daily struggle
And entered 'gates of gold'
We'll cherish every memory
Remembering days of old

Loved one,
You are with us forever
Never forgotten
Immortal loved one

# CHAPTER TWO

## SUNDOWN
### HEALING

## HEALING

Surrender

Change

Acceptance

Hope

Humanity has come a long way...

A far and long way from how we used to treat each
other: a gesture of kindness, basic courtesy of a
smile, and whatever happened to *community*?
Most of us do not even know our neighbors.

Seems everyone is too busy searching for solutions,
freedom, happiness, serenity, relief.

# POETRY IN THE AIR

...She breathes poetry

She arrived uninvited
With a plan undivided
Her agenda: Live happy. Live free.

An observer of faces, of feelings
Of untimely times and faraway places
An unshakeable will to explore
To survive, a rose garden of life
Refreshing, alive

To be adorned and adored
In a dream-like abode
Sit refined as a shiny wife-trophy
Spend each day kitchen bound
On a merry-go-round
Watching others parade duty-free?
A condition far worse than a
Hermit's curse
Startled, she yelled,
"Not for me!"

She heard the rumors of
Cold, barren lands
News of so many
Good men turned bad

"We have only one chance
In this life full of strife
There was only one plan:
*Send relief*!
The people are troubled
Let us help them cope
If only for moments
Spread harmony and hope
See an end to the madness
The conflict, the pain
Stop poverty and waste
Extinguish the flames
End children's sadness
Suffering, strain
Help arid lands turn to
A flourish green...

...to hear once again good Earth sing,"

Now THAT is a beautiful thing!

She breathes poetry...

# KARMA AFTERTHOUGHTS

The lessons would
Certainly arrive
Be understood
A little too late

The ongoing war
Between left and right
Shoulder angels
Both left in wonderment
Who will win today's
Moral argument?

Your actions did not seem like
Such a big deal at the time
The chain of events set in motion
Unstoppable as a clock's chime

Now, reality is nothing but
A haunting memory
Regret is your constant companion
It's a hamster wheel of reminders:

How long before becoming
   Older
     Wiser
       Happy again?

## RIPPLE'S HALT

One glass
Two glass
Three glass, four
Don't think I can
Drive
Better to lie here
On this floor
Than to never once again
Go home

    "Glasses,
      Glasses,
      We all
      Fall down!"

Whew! Glad I stopped myself
That could have been my last one

Behold, protect and cherish the temple
That is you: A MASTERPIECE
Years in the making

Take back your health
Take back control
To love yourself is to love your family too

*Wine, I love you, but I love my family more*
*Wine, I need you, but my family needs me more*
*Goodbye sweet wine!*
*There is a place for you*
*But not here, not now*
*A newer, stronger, healthier version of me is on*
*the way, because I love my family*
*- And I love me too -*
*I will put the wine away*

Time. To. Halt. The. Wine.

# SURRENDER

Fate will bring you good fortune
Fate will take it away
It is not until you take a ride
On MORTALITY ROAD
Stare death in the face
Veil of serenity pulled
You stand alone
Vulnerable
Shaken to the core
When you suddenly realize
None of this is under your control
Once your eyes have seen the
Reality of life's finality
The waterfall of
Unstoppable tears
Joy extinguished, emptied
From life's harsh blows
Your world
Spinning out of control
No energy left
Not even to
Explode

Let the river of life flow
Just let go...
The sunlight will return
Have a little faith
Renewal will arrive, like
Springtime's perfect timing
You will more than survive

When it seems darkest, life will teach you:
*Inner-strength*
  *Endurance*
    *Compassion*
    *Wisdom*
    *Patience*

Surrender
It is a mysterious and quiet process
No effort needed whatsoever
You will overcome
You will grow
Understand, and
You will glow...
So let the river of life flow

Say it.

Think it.

Let go.

Feel it.

**R e l i e f**

Repeat

# TABLE FOR ONE

What would you give
For a hot cup of tea
On a cold winter's night
As you wearily flee
From the grip that engulfs
And the tone that berates
You're much better alone
You're your own best
Soul mate

## VIBES

People think their impulsive words
Crass loudness and brash behavior
Have no effect on others

Like dandelion seeds that spread
In all directions, so too are the
Emotions you emit, radiating
Far-reaching after-effects

Don't believe me
I'm nobody
Test it for yourself
On your parent
In the street
Frown at a stranger
See what you get back
I hope they aren't impulsive
I hope they don't attack


Now, *smile* at a total stranger
Or a not-so-pretty girl
Give a smiling glance at a
Wrinkled soul...

*-It made you smile too-*


YOU'VE JUST IMPROVED THE WORLD!

# UNWIND

Winding through the Eucalyptus and
Pine, maneuvering past majestic Redwoods
Enjoying the curves of the road, the
Trail was thick with harmony and fresh air;
Sweet fresh air into wind-tossed hair

The roar of the river
The hum of nature's music
Relaxing your frame
Like a deep massage
Free for all who choose it

The clean and peaceful aromatic scents
Of calm, deep Redwood offerings
The waft of soothing Eucalyptus leaves
These are sanity's most beneficial things

Euphoric as a tantalizing first glance
A ride through the fresh woods becomes
The most revitalizing trance

Behold the scents that heal
Awakening your mind
Into crystal-clear focus
Refreshing your soul into a natural high
The wonders of nature, of unharmed forests
Furthest from land scorched dry

THIS IS THE LEGENDARY MEDICINE
OF OUR FOREFATHERS

The trees...the breeze...the sun...the ease

# WAKE UP YOUR INNER GREAT

We're all used to doing things
The same old way
Together we can change the world
Rid the bad of yesterday

Let go of all excuses
Decide once and for all
Stick to the right decisions
Standing proudly, standing tall

If only I could right the wrongs
If only they could hear my songs
We'd put an end to tragedies
There wouldn't be such misery

No such thing as a mean baby
Never one was born to hate
Imitate and teach the children
To love, forgive, and appreciate

I'm talking about our young ones
Those that grow up way too fast
It's our job to teach and guide them
Shielding them from evil's blast

Let's never give up, no, never let up
This new world is ours to shape
But time's not stopping
And evil's still hopping...

WAKE UP YOUR INNER GREAT!

## WILL WE EVER BE UNITED?

It's time for a change
To free our young ones
To live without fear
Of hovering guns

The governing rules
Will shave off our hair
Reducing our strength
To a pitiful snare

Immobile and helpless
They want us to stay
Cause if we stay silent
We'll wither away...

The voice that's inside you
So humble and quiet
Let's send out our message
Without making riots

Don't look at my income
Don't label my skin
Imagine with eyes closed
We're practically twins

We're all the same package
Our lifeblood within
This DNA blessing
One family, one kin

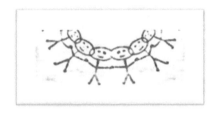

Will we ever be united?
Letting go of racial slurs
Nations see we're so divided
Let's make hate a faded blur

# A TRUE HERO

There are so many heroes
Humble, unsung heroes
A true hero will not always be the one
Dressed in uniform, they come in all colors
All sizes; some help feed the hungry, others
Head straight for the storm

You'll find them in each city
Small towns, nondescript places
You've probably already met
Their nonchalant faces
Some weathered, aged
Others strong, young
With young families
Counting on them
Be it distant or near
Ready and willing for
The cue to embark
A person with a loving
Compassionate heart
Non-egotistical, thrust into
Imminent danger, saving
The life of a total stranger

They gather from all walks of life
Some seek work that fulfills a calling
Danger does not stop them
Nor will it ever cause a stalling
Courage appears at the burst of
Life's happy bubble
They secretly live for the
Thrill of thwarting trouble

A true hero will never ask for a cent
Nor a pat on the back, though they'll
Give the shirt off their back; nor
Recognition for a job well spent
They know they may not make it out alive
Giving us all a second chance at life

UNPREDICTABLE is the way of the world
Keep your fingers crossed you
Don't cross the wrong path
Be kind to others
It might save your soul
If your luck runs out:
You're in luck with a hero

Finding a hero is not so difficult, and if you look
closely, you might be surprised...there exists a hero
in every family, every community, perhaps
someone who has always been there for you; it
might even be the person in the mirror; or it could
be someone who is older, seen as weak, yet capable
of marvelous feats.

*** 

My kids are my heroes.
They give me strength when I've none left.
More than a vitamin.
More than a pep talk.

It doesn't matter whether or not they have a
degree, or a low-paying or high-paying job,
if they're unemployed, or even locked up...
Whether or not they call daily or hardly...
My kids make me feel like I'm the most loved
mother in the world. That is why, no matter what
life brings my way, I am satisfied. I have it all.

***

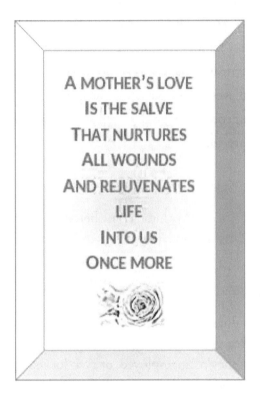

A MOTHER'S LOVE
IS THE SALVE
THAT NURTURES
ALL WOUNDS
AND REJUVENATES
LIFE
INTO US
ONCE MORE

# MY MOTHER'S LOVE

FOR MY ONE AND ONLY:

When a storm comes into
Our fragile lives
You are the calm
Shielding us
Before, during, and after
Making sense of life's disasters

One hug from you
Sweet mother and
I feel complete protection
A relief from all my troubles
When badness strikes
From all directions

Nothing else can compare
I hope to be there for you
As you have been for me
But seems I'm always chained
Behind a life so far from easy

My whole world changed
When distance arrived
Now, far away, there is
Nothing I could do or
Say to make you stay

It is the simplest moments
I miss the most
Every reunion with you
Is a sacred celebration
Pure quality time
A reason for elation
I want to include us both
In my plans at Forever Station

Know you are ingrained
Deep in my heart
Like Siamese twins
We must have been
Will always be
Together and forever
As canvassed art

"Pardon Mama"
Emile Munier. 1888
Public Domain, CCO 1.0

# SCARS, BRUISES AND FAITH

Why do the scars on my face
Bother you more than me...
Does it mar me into imperfection?
Did it ruin your ideal image of me?
Does it frighten you like a zombie?

These scars do not define who I am
They taught me to be tough
Never let your guard down
Always there as a warning
Be ready for anything

I am still the same person
I was before the scars
And if I had a dozen more
I would still be the same soul
Same mind, same heart

Because who I am goes deeper than
Skin
 Flesh
  Bone
   Image
    Personality
An invisible light occupying
A physical temple
A surging force
A testimony
A gift of life energy
Experiencing humanity
Running, learning endlessly

It took me a long time to realize
My spirit will live on
Quietly reserved
After my living flesh rests
Why then, such a short life?
Why this unquenchable, ongoing
Thirst for knowledge?

And with this
Never-ending
Desire for learning,
A deep, natural
Instinctive, heartfelt
Yearning to live
ETERNALLY
(Where did that come from?)
I wondered for years...

Then, it occurred to me:
They promised us a resurrection
Of people, not zombies
No. That would be sci-fi
The zombie resurrection
Is a blatant lie
I speak of something beautiful
An old promise of hope
Of a new life
How do I explain such a
Complex belief?

I still don't have the words to explain
What my eyes-mind-heart
Have seen-learned-felt

It is something you must search for...
Want deeply—ask for—a special request
A yearning for discernment

I do know this:

    Trials
    Tribulations
    Signs
    Messages
    Path
    Tests
    Endurance
    Coincidences
    Miracles
    Good fortune
    Bad fortune

...can lead to faith

Each one of us is here for a reason
With so much generosity and need
Accept the gifts that you are given
Share and just say no to greed

The question is
When you finally take
All that life gives
Will it change you for the better?
Will you use it for good?

Or

Will you sum it all up
To luck, chance, or waste?
Will it perish in your haste?
Will you continue to see only
What your physical eyes see?

Sometimes
    Not seeing
        Is believing

# SOUNDS OF CHANGE

It was a sound like no other...
A sound that would not, could not be ignored, not by me, nor any other person watching, listening, and standing in the local shopping center parking lot on that autumn day...

A sound only heard in movies. Not even in film can you create the chill that rattles your bones and sickens the pit of your stomach for what is inevitably to follow...

It must have lasted about 30 seconds--the longest 30 seconds of my life...all eyes fixated on the white SUV careening out of control, whose sound was a desperation to stop, and a confession of high velocity guilt. An out-of-place, unexpected chain of events. A 'Twilight-Zone' bizarre moment...

Did the young man giving away phones know that this day would be his last day of work? Never.

Did the two ladies who had just shopped, waiting for a bus--did they know a car would come for them instead? Not a clue. How strange, I thought, we take our sweet time planning our days, then the sound of chaos erupts, and life as we know it changes forever...

I could no longer shop for that much needed sweater for the cold fall mornings that had arrived. Too jolted to continue shopping, I was magnetically drawn towards the scene of the accident.

Where did all these people come from? Car parts and debris were scattered everywhere. The helicopter, ambulance and media crew arrived quickly. It was like the nightmare you never awaken from, no one can see or hear you, and you're at the center of it all trying to wake up.

The expression on the officer's face as he did CPR was a mixture of exasperation, hope and pain. He was soon motioned by another officer, the one who took the victim's pulse, to stop, swaying his head left-to-right. The black drape of death was quietly summoned.

I had never before watched anyone die. I looked around and sensed it was up to me to say a prayer. Just then, a breeze of calm swept by on this otherwise windless day, then, like a meticulously planned movie scene, the sun shone its angled ray on the body, I blinked, it was gone. Did I hallucinate?

The officer knelt next to the body. This was not the same type of kneeling as when an officer kneels on a suspects' jugular – no –it was a slow, respectful type of kneeling, the type you see when a soldier carefully, lovingly lays to rest a beloved president.

I grew still. Once the shock wore off, peace and tranquility came over me. Vanished were the years of deeply-rooted anger I harbored towards cops. I realized that while there are some bad apples in the police force, who was I to sentence and judge every officer as corrupt? And even though my sons had been targeted and judged and sentenced as such, I could not continue to do the same.

At that moment, I realized why the universe had put me there: At the wrong place, and at the wrong time. Because it was the *right* place at the *right* time. It is only in the silence of pain that I have learned to listen well.

As the late Martin Luther King Jr. once said, "Hate is too heavy a burden to carry."

Lighten your load.
Now is the beginning of the healing of our soul.

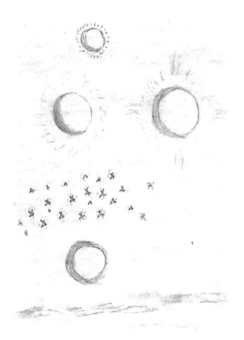

# THE SECOND COMING

He is coming again
In the stronghold of the wind
Through the twinkling of a star
For him, *far* is not that far

See, he's always been in wait
Waiting for his time to state
For a time it seemed too late
In a world that loves to hate

He'll return and just amaze
A million angels on his side
All that's wrong will be
Set straight
Once they open
Heaven's gate

He is coming again...
I can't wait

# SUNDOWN

Goodnight day light
*Adios* sea shore
Respected light
Return

Away go madness
Goodnight sorrow
I rest on comforts
I've prayers to borrow

I pray we get
Another day
A chance to make
Amends
Before the final
Curtain call
Before the lonely
Darkness falls
Just one other
Chance is all...

Then, all begins again...

# CHAPTER THREE

## SUNRISE

### CELEBRATION

# CELEBRATION

Awaken

Explore

Blossom

Delight

## SUNRISE

Under universal orchestra
Our loving solar gem emerges
A floating, stark-bright radiance
Giving warmth and life in surges

Dressed in molten golden armor
Adorned a burnt-red halo
Onward moving towards daylight
Our one true luminary sight

Like the morning glory of a singing bird
Or the alarm of a commanding siren
A dependable and daily greeting
Of a salutation seldom silent

Awakening the mountain lions
Then a slow and slumbering sloth
Next, the pleasing showy opening act
Of a handsome feathered male peacock

Energizing hummingbirds
Oceans, hawks, and doves
Feeding large voluptuous ferns
The palm, the river, and everyone with love

Stretching outwardly towards infinity
Radiates the bursting brilliance
Of a million diamonds in the breeze
Stands forever in resilience

## POETRY'S RENAISSANCE

Solitary soul,
Like a trampled pebble on
A long, crowded shore
A thousand tales inside you
*A million to one, that's your number*

A stranger to peace
Crashing waves never rest
Nor wind nor Earth's constant
Need for a quest
To replenish, restore
Return once more
*You strike with the fury of thunder*

Outdated murmur of a cynics' decree
Faded whispers of old poetry's eulogy
Outspoken now is the emerging chant:
 *Sweep away, rise, end of the slumber!*

Of Chaucer, and Homer
Of dear Shakespeare's lore
Outshined by a new dawn of arrival
There's more...
A new season of reason
Of bright colors so pleasing
 *At last, came awaited revival*

This new feeling's delightfully
Winning, inspiration brings
On new beginnings
Winds of fortune and ease
Renaissance in the breeze
 *Here's a gift filled with more*
 *Than a grinning*

# PANDEMIC'S END

"Now there isn't much time
As these things were foretold
Earthquakes, war, floods, and swine
From that book that's so old

So many lives gone now
A memory, a haze
Who'd have guessed that a cough
Would cut short our days?

We gathered at warp speed
The best in the nation
An army of soldiers
Worked in collaboration

Where once left and right
Were at polarized ends
But for mankind's survival
We're making amends."

Our fight for survival continues...
It never seems to end; with each new dawn
Comes a different, menacing disaster
The hand-of-time gave us a penny of luck
Friend or foes, we need each other
More than ever, we come to depend on our
Televisions just to hear a friendly voice
While counting casualties

For a rare, silent moment in time
We heard each other's voices
Understood, without speaking
Apart and distant, yet, united
What separated us also brought us together, and

In the middle of our universal stormy sunshine, of
what seemed our greatest threat and challenge, we
connected, created a chain of effort, empathy, and
became heroes to each other.

Yes, it seems we can get along after all.
If we try.

CORONARIA BLOOMS

Meet

# Coronaria

**A flower representing**

**The end of cold, dark days**

**And the return of the sun**

**I invited her to stay**

# DESPAIR TO REPAIR

A newer, kinder generation emerged
Typically not in the spotlight
They are the quiet ones
With a desire to change the old
Selfish, greedy, toxic path
That led to this grand mess

Their young eyes beam light of hope
For an upheld Public Trust Doctrine
A guarantee to see a better future
Advocating for the smartest solutions
Before the tipping point arrives
Wasting no more time
On the train called
THE DISASTER LINE
In a peaceful revolution

"Step away from the insanity,"
Einstein said it best.
Grab your dose of opportunity
Prepare for better days ahead

Hope, unity, communication:
Their strength

Understanding:
Their philosophy

Sharing, solving, and caring:
Their way of life

Truth:
Their shield of defense

Happiness is the reward, and
They stand welcoming all
Arms wide open

-21 Kids against the Government

## BLANK CANVAS

Here you are again
Thinking about
The opportunities gone
A million things undone
Days left, never to return

Far from your ideal life?

Open your mind
Today is that day
You create the agenda
Fill in your blank canvas
Prepare it for tomorrow

Do it while you can
Because it is only

**Time**

We can never borrow

S till nothing on the agenda?

A blank canvas of
No ideas
No job
No destination?

You no longer have to wait
Permission to play has been granted
Time to laugh, move, create
Elevate to a higher state

Don't look back at sorrows
Better days are on the way
Your personal blank canvas
Renews itself each day

# HATS

## Every Day It Rains Hats

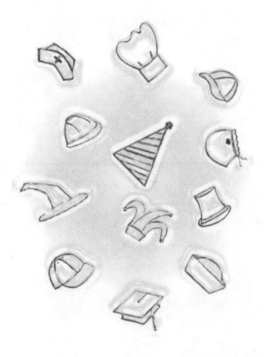

# Which one will you
# Wear today?

"Bubba bear likes the party hat"

## SILLY POETRY

Why do I keep writing

My silly poetry?

Who really gives a damn

Damn poetry slam

Just another

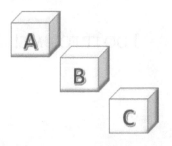

*"An avid listener is my journal,*

*A place to purge my soul's internal."*

OH YEAH

THAT'S RIGHT

I DO IT FOR ME!

# RECIPE FOR A GREAT DAY

Take from your memory bank those happiest,
brightest moments dear to your heart; like a
cherished time capsule, locked in your vault of
knowledge, yours alone, this can never be taken:
> Treasures from the heart

Recall the smiles of loved ones on a warm summer
day under the blue sky as you jumped into the
seashore, seagulls flying above; joy, laughter and
song, all day long:
> Treasures from the heart

The blessings and warmth of loved ones at the
unforgettable gathering when you couldn't stop
laughing at the silly joke that really wasn't that
funny at all, it was the sheer delight of being in the
company of those you love most:
> Treasures from the heart

Recall the joy you felt when you gave a much-
needed gift to a total stranger, their look of
appreciation; or the inquiring glance of a true
friend's concern; or the visit of one who never
questions your absence, no matter how many years
have passed:

Treasures from the heart

Hold on to these
kind thoughts
as a reminder that
you are loved, cherished,
and remembered,
for you already hold
the recipe to happiness
in your very own heart.

# WHY WRITE?

Every word is free
They're at your fingertips
No need to pay a fee
Don't need to take a trip

Just look into your heart
What emotions do you feel?
Use your imagination
It doesn't all have to be real

In thinking of the issues that
Cause you to lose sleep
While all are deep in slumber
Through the darkness, you do creep

Your hand can't wait to write it
As new ideas unfold
Your mind is bubbling daydreams
Capture "it" before it goes

It goes away, away
Like a helium balloon
Like the fireworks that fade
Under darkness of a moon

Like dewdrops under sun fire
That will surely disappear
So keep pen and paper handy
Your immortality lies here

# BEACON OF LIGHT

You

And your pen...

Writing words

That become

The light that shines

Upon those whose

Lives are dim

With sorrow,

You are

Their hope

For a

Brighter

Tomorrow

# "DON'T TELL ME WHAT

# I NEED TO WRITE

# !

# I'M WRITING WHAT

# I NEED TO TELL"

-Teenage-like, rebellious, writer's passion

## POETRY'S FINEST HOUR

Does anybody really know
How to grasp sunlight's prose?
For our short time on Earth
Who will fulfill poetry's girth?

Are we bold enough to unmask
Our deepest, guarded feelings?
And if we move forward with the task
Will it be worthy of revealing?

Will it be as sweet as a puppy at play?
Will the words make them laugh or cry
Inspire others to gallop in the rain
Will it bring pleasure or pain?

Will it be like streaming water
That floats away, away...
Or a quick passing fancy, as
The flavor of the day?

Will it last long
Like a classic love song
Like iron and steel
Stand solid and strong

Taste it like candy
Delectable and sweet
Poetry and verse:
Life's two worthy treats

With internal power
An abundant word shower
Endless and vast as
Eternity's tower

Where every fine poet
Gives words to devour
We have now entered
Poetry's finest hour.

# ATTRIBUTION & CREDITS

Alvarado, Regina Medina, Why Write, "The Best Poems & Poets of 2007," edited by Howard Ely, The International Library of Poetry, 2008, page 1.

Aztec Princess Illustration gifted to Regina Medina Alvarado by unknown artist. 2010.

Cover designed in CANVA under the CANVA free and proContentDAFdmmNgE8s/ xZx4Va9loAIEF2_ g5V0azg/view?utm_content=DAFdmmNgE8s&utm_campaign=share_your_design&utm_medium =link&utm_source=shareyourdesignpanel License Agreement. Access date March 25, 2023.

Munier, Emile. *Pardon Mama*. 1888. Image. CCO 1.0. http://nevsepic.com.ua/art-i-risovanaya-grafika/page,3,7649-francuzskiy-hudozhnik-emile-munier-1840-1895-94-rabot.html, Public Domain, https://commons.wikimedia.org/w/index.php?cur id=36746391. Access date: 01-08-2023

Open Font License Fonts used: AR Julian at Fontstera.com/pcappstore standard license/ar-julian-font/, Carlito SIL OPEN FONT LICENSE Version 1.1 - 26 February 2007, Julius Sans One SIL OPEN FONT LICENSE Version 1.1 - 26 February 2007, and EB Garamond under the SIL OPEN FONT LICENSE Version 1.1 - 26 February 2007.

# ACKNOWLEDGEMENTS

I would like to extend my heartfelt gratitude to all self-published poets, and to the many website authors who provide free information, tools, and knowledge. Your tenacity in removing the barriers that poets have been subject to for so long through the difficult wall of publishing has eased the road for everyone. This book would not have been possible without your efforts.

Now, poets all over the world have access to what was formerly limited to a select few. Thank you for reviving poetry into our modern literature and arts scene. The world is now a better place.

# AUTHOR'S NOTE

Poetry has been on a long journey. It has stood as a vital force in literature since the dawn of writing. Mention the word "poetry," and most people think of William Shakespeare (1567-1616), or Edgar Allen Poe (1809-1849), to name a few.

Early poets were trailblazers that set a path for all future poets, and left us with a taste of what life was like in their day. They paved the way.

Today, poets do not write in "old" English or Elizabethan style; however, the stigma has remained. For that reason, some are hesitant to read today's poetry.

Poetry is alive, well, and new again. It has made a favorable comeback, taking front and center stage with poets all over the world filling the spotlight. Readers connect with poets and their poems in the universal language of emotion and need for expression.

Who is to say how much our writings and our language will evolve in 200, 300 or 1000 years? How many new words will be created? How many of our modern words and phrases will fade away into textbook history?

Only time will tell.

This is our time to make our mark. The gigantic welcome sign is up. We have entered a new era of poetic expression and freedom. The poems inside you are waiting to jump onto the page.

Your journey has just begun...
Poetry's journey has just begun.

-RMA

# AUTHOR BIO

Regina Medina Alvarado is a Northern Californian who always knew growing up she would become a poet. It wasn't easy to escape the echoes of her grammar school teachers' voices telling her, "Regina Medina, you are a poet!"

Never a poet by profession, she finally found enough quiet time to share her poetry with the world.

She encourages anyone who has ever wanted to write poetry, stories, a memoir, a self-help book, or a novel to begin. Write. Just write. The rest will fall into place. One page at a time.

**Get more poetry on:**

## International
## Poetry Day
March 21
Annually
Worldwide

## National Poetry Month
In the United States
The month of April

## Random Acts of
## Poetry Day
First Wednesday of October
Encouraging outbursts of poetry
Spoken or left written in visible areas
To spread the art of poetry

Made in United States
Troutdale, OR
04/04/2024

18933500R00105